Davis

by Iain Gray

WRITING *to* REMEMBER

79 Main Street, Newtongrange,
Midlothian EH22 4NA
Tel: 0131 344 0414   Fax: 0845 075 6085
E-mail: info@lang-syne.co.uk
www.langsyneshop.co.uk

Design by Dorothy Meikle
Printed by Printwell Ltd
© Lang Syne Publishers Ltd 2022

All rights reserved. No part of this publication may be reproduced, stored or introduced into a retrieval system, or transmitted in any form or by any means (electronic, mechanical, photocopying, recording or otherwise) without the prior written permission of Lang Syne Publishers Ltd.

ISBN 978-1-85217-781-2

Davis

MOTTO:
Without God, without anything

CREST:
A lion

TERRITORY:
Flintshire

NAME variations include:
Daves
Davies
Dafis
Dafys
Davidson
Davie
Davison
Divis
Dawson

Chapter one:
The origins of popular surnames

by George Forbes and Iain Gray

If you don't know where you came from, you won't know where you're going **is a frequently quoted observation and one that has a particular resonance today when there has been a marked upsurge in interest in genealogy, with increasing numbers of people curious to trace their family roots.**

Main sources for genealogical research include census returns and official records of births, marriages and deaths – and the key to unlocking the detail they contain is obviously a family surname, one that has been 'inherited' and passed from generation to generation.

No matter our station in life, we all have a surname – but it was not until about the middle of the fourteenth century that the practice of being identified by a particular surname became commonly established throughout the British Isles.

Previous to this, it was normal for a person to be identified through the use of only a forename.

But as population gradually increased and there were many more people with the same forename, surnames were adopted to distinguish one person, or community, from another.

Many common English surnames are patronymic in origin, meaning they stem from the forename of one's father – with 'Johnson,' for example, indicating 'son of John.'

It was the Normans, in the wake of their eleventh century conquest of Anglo-Saxon England, a pivotal moment in the nation's history, who first brought surnames into usage – although it was a gradual process.

For the Normans, these were names initially based on the title of their estates, local villages and chateaux in France to distinguish and identify these landholdings.

Such grand descriptions also helped enhance the prestige of these warlords and generally glorify their lofty positions high above the humble serfs slaving away below in the pecking order who had only single names, often with Biblical connotations as in Pierre and Jacques.

The only descriptive distinctions among the peasantry concerned their occupations, like 'Pierre the swineherd' or 'Jacques the ferryman.'

Roots of surnames that came into usage in England not only included Norman-French, but also Old French, Old Norse, Old English, Middle English, German, Latin, Greek, Hebrew and the Gaelic languages of the Celts.

The Normans themselves were originally Vikings, or 'Northmen', who raided, colonised and eventually settled down around the French coastline.

They had sailed up the Seine in their long-boats in 900AD under their ferocious leader Rollo and ruled the roost in north eastern France before sailing over to conquer England in 1066 under Duke William of Normandy – better known to posterity as William the Conqueror, or King William I of England.

Granted lands in the newly-conquered England, some of their descendants later acquired territories in Wales, Scotland and Ireland – taking not only their own surnames, but also the practice of adopting a surname, with them.

But it was in England where Norman rule and custom first impacted, particularly in relation to the adoption of surnames.

This is reflected in the famous *Domesday Book*, a massive survey of much of England and Wales, ordered by William I, to determine who owned what, what it was worth and therefore how much they were liable to pay in taxes to the voracious Royal Exchequer.

Completed in 1086 and now held in the National Archives in Kew, London, 'Domesday' was an Old English word meaning 'Day of Judgement.'

This was because, in the words of one contemporary chronicler, "its decisions, like those of the Last Judgement, are unalterable."

It had been a requirement of all those English landholders – from the richest to the poorest – that they identify themselves for the purposes of the survey and for future reference by means of a surname.

This is why the *Domesday Book*, although written in Latin as was the practice for several centuries with both civic and ecclesiastical records, is an invaluable source for the early appearance of a wide range of English surnames.

Several of these names were coined in connection with occupations.

These include Baker and Smith, while Cooks, Chamberlains, Constables and Porters were to be found carrying out duties in large medieval households.

The church's influence can be found in names such as Bishop, Friar and Monk while the popular name of Bennett derives from the late fifth to mid-sixth century Saint Benedict, founder of the Benedictine order of monks.

The early medical profession is represented by Barber, while businessmen produced names that include Merchant and Sellers.

Down at the village watermill, the names that cropped up included Millar/Miller, Walker and Fuller, while other self-explanatory trades included Cooper, Tailor, Mason and Wright.

Even the scenery was utilised as in Moor, Hill, Wood and Forrest – while the hunt and the chase supplied names that include Hunter, Falconer, Fowler and Fox.

Colours are also a source of popular surnames, as in Black, Brown, Gray/Grey, Green and White, and would have denoted the colour of the clothing the person habitually wore or, apart from the obvious exception of 'Green', one's hair colouring or even complexion.

The surname Red developed into Reid, while

Blue was rare and no-one wanted to be associated with yellow.

Rather self-important individuals took surnames that include Goodman and Wiseman, while physical attributes crept into surnames such as Small and Little.

Many families proudly boast the heraldic device known as a Coat of Arms, as featured on our front cover.

The central motif of the Coat of Arms would originally have been what was borne on the shield of a warrior to distinguish himself from others on the battlefield.

Not featured on the Coat of Arms, but highlighted on page three, is the family motto and related crest – with the latter frequently different from the central motif.

Adding further variety to the rich cultural heritage that is represented by surnames is the appearance in recent times in lists of the 100 most common names found in England of ones that include Khan, Patel and Singh – names that have proud roots in the vast sub-continent of India.

Echoes of a far distant past can still be found in our surnames and they can be borne with pride in commemoration of our forebears.

Chapter two:

Of royal pedigree

A name of ancient roots, 'Davis' is ranked 56th in some lists of the 100 most common surnames found throughout the United Kingdom today, but it is in Wales that it is particularly prevalent.

Derived from the popular personal name David and indicating 'son of David' or 'son of St David', it is of Biblical roots, meaning 'beloved' and also the name of the Old Testament David, founder of the Jewish Royal House of David.

The name also became popularised in medieval times through veneration for St David, the mid to late sixth century Welsh bishop later canonised as a saint and adopted as the patron saint of Wales.

With a white dove as his emblem, he was a renowned preacher and teacher and founded a number of churches and monastic settlements that include what is now St David's Cathedral, in Pembrokeshire, on the site of one of the monasteries he founded.

While many bearers of common surnames found in the United Kingdom today are of Anglo-

Saxon roots, bearers of the Davis name are of even earlier Brythonic, or British, origin.

Of Celtic pedigree, these early inhabitants of the British Isles were settled for centuries from a line south of the River Forth in Scotland all the way down to the south coast of England and with a particular presence in Wales.

Speaking a Celtic language known as Brythonic, they boasted a glorious culture that flourished even after the Roman invasion of Britain in 43 AD and the subsequent consolidation of Roman power by about 84 AD.

With many of the original Britons absorbing aspects of Roman culture, they became 'Romano-British' – while still retaining their own proud Celtic heritage, and some of the name today can claim a descent from a royal prince.

This is through the late twelfth century Cynrig Efell, Lord of Eglwsegle, a twin son of Madog ap Maredudd, the last prince of the Welsh kingdom of Powys.

An ancient legend is that Madog, who died in 1160, had somehow discovered America centuries before Christopher Columbus – and there was an upsurge in interest in this in the late eighteenth century.

The legend goes even further, claiming that there was actually a tribe of 'Welsh' Indians, descended from those who had accompanied Madog on his discovery of America.

The Davis name, along with its equally popular spelling variant of 'Davies' is particularly associated with modern day Flintshire, known in Welsh as *Sir y Fflint*, in the north east of Wales and which was once part of the mighty kingdom of Gwynedd.

In common with other ancient Welsh kingdoms, it fell victim to the Normans following their Conquest of England in 1066 and later to the ambitious and ruthless King Edward I.

Duke William II of Normandy was declared King of England two months after his invasion, and the complete subjugation of his Anglo-Saxon subjects followed, with those Normans who had fought on his behalf rewarded with lands – a pattern that would be followed in Wales.

Invading across the Welsh Marches, the borderland between England and Wales, they gradually consolidated their gains.

But, under a succession of Welsh leaders who included Llywelyn ap Gruffudd, known as Llywelyn the Last, resistance proved strong.

Llwelyn's uprising was brutally crushed in 1283 under Edward I, who ordered the building or repair of at least 17 castles and in 1302 proclaimed his son and heir, the future King Edward II, as Prince of Wales, a title known in Welsh as *Tywysog Cymru*.

Another heroic Welsh figure dominated the struggle from 1400 to 1415 in the form of Owain Glyndŵr – the last native Welshman to be recognised by his supporters as *Tywysog Cymru*.

In what is known as The Welsh Revolt he achieved an early series of stunning victories against King Henry IV and his successor Henry V – until mysteriously disappearing from the historical record after mounting an ambush in Brecon.

One particularly colourful seventeenth century bearer of the Davis name was Mary Davis, the singer, actress, courtesan and mistress of King Charles II better known to posterity as Moll Davis.

Born in the Westminster area of London in about 1648, her parentage is not known with any degree of certainty, although some sources suggest she may have been an illegitimate daughter of Thomas Howard, 3rd Earl of Berkshire.

Taking to the London stage in the early 1660s, she became a popular entertainer with the

Duke's Theatre Company with a flair for acting, singing, dancing and comedy.

It was either in this theatre or in a coffee house that in 1667 she first made the acquaintance of Charles II, seven years after his Restoration to the throne.

Infatuated with her, he showered her with gifts that, according to the contemporary diarist Samuel Pepys, included a "mighty pretty fine coach" and a ring worth £600 – a vast sum in those times.

Flaunting the wealth she acquired through being the king's mistress – although she was only one of a number of ladies, including Nell Gwynn, whose favours the king enjoyed – she also acquired a reputation for 'vulgarity and greed' and certainly did not lack for detractors.

Pepys' wife, for example, described her as "the most impertinent slut in the world."

Giving up the stage about a year after being set up as the king's mistress she had a child by him – the future Lady Mary Tudor.

It was perhaps through the machinations of her bitter rival for the king's favour, Nell Gwynn, that Charles ended the relationship in about 1672.

But the severance came with financial

compensation – as he granted her an annual pension for life of £1,000 and also lavishly furnished a house for her.

Noting this, Pepys remarked how the house was furnished "most richly, which is an infinite shame."

The subject of portraits by the fashionable society artist Sir Peter Lely, in 1686 she married the celebrated French musician and composer James Paisible and, when Charles II's successor King James II was forced to flee into French exile during the 'Glorious Revolution' of 1688, the couple joined his court-in-exile at St Germain-en-Laye.

Returning to England with her husband in 1693, she died in 1708.

Chapter three:

Science and discovery

Bearers of the Davis name have gained both fame and infamy on the high seas.

One who gained the former was the sixteenth century English navigator John Davis, who not only led a number of voyages during the reign of Queen Elizabeth I to discover the elusive Northwest Passage, but also discovered the Falkland Islands.

Born in about 1550 in Stoke Gabriel, Devon, but spending his childhood in Sandridge, Hertfordshire, he first took to sea at an early age.

By 1585 his navigational skills were such that he was able to persuade the queen's secretary, Francis Walsingham, to back what became a number of attempts to find the Northwest Passage.

Not discovered until 1850, this is a sea route that connects the Northern Atlantic and Pacific oceans along the northern coast of North America.

But although Davis' attempts proved abortive, they were nevertheless valuable in terms of general maritime exploration.

Discoveries he made on his voyages, in

addition to the discovery of the Falkland Islands in 1592, aboard the vessel *Desire*, include the charting of what is now named in his honour as the Davis Inlet on the coast of Labrador.

But tragedy struck in 1605, when he was killed by a Japanese pirate whose vessel he had just seized off Bintan Island, Singapore.

His legacy endures, however, through his invention of the navigational aid the back staff and double quadrant – named the Davis Quadrant – while his important works on navigation include his 1594 *The Seaman's Secrets* and, published a year later, *The World's Hydrographical Description*.

Still on the high seas, but on an infamous note, Captain Howell Davis was the Welsh pirate who, in a piratical career that lasted just under one year, captured at least fifteen English and French ships.

Born in about 1690 in Milford Haven, Pembrokeshire, he had been serving as a mate in July of 1718 aboard the slave ship *Cadogan* when it was captured by pirates.

Opting to join their ranks, the pirate captain gave him command of the *Cadogan* and he set sail for Brazil.

But his crew mutinied and the *Cadogan* sailed instead to Barbados, where Davis was promptly arrested and imprisoned on charges of piracy.

Released for reasons that remain unclear, he headed for New Providence, in the Bahamas, later leaving in the sloop *Buck* – promptly mutinying along with other crew members and taking control of the vessel.

A brief, but lucrative, piratical career followed—it included the capture of the 26-gun *Saint James* and the 32-gun *Rover*.

But his exploits came to an end in June of 1719 when, attempting to kidnap and hold to ransom the governor of the Portuguese island of Principe, he was ambushed and shot dead.

From the high seas to the worlds of medicine and the sciences, David Davis, born in 1777 in Llandyfaelog, was the Welsh physician who served as a royal obstetrician.

Graduating in medicine from Glasgow University in 1801, he set up a medical practice in Sheffield before moving to London to take up the post of 'physician accoucher' at the Queen Charlotte Lying-in Hospital.

It was in this role that he attended the

Duchess of Kent when she gave birth to the future Queen Victoria in 1819.

A pioneer of obstetrics and the author of a number of textbook works on the subject, he died in 1841.

Regarded as the founding father of the scientific discipline of chemical engineering, Edward George Davis was born in 1850 in Eton, Berkshire.

The son of a bookseller, he was apprenticed as a bookbinder when aged 14, but abandoned this in favour of his passion for science.

Following studies at institutions that included the Royal School of Mines, London – now part of Imperial College – he was an inspector for the Alkali Act of 1863 that sought to reduce the amount of gaseous hydrochloric acid released into the atmosphere from the chimneys of soda manufacturers.

Focussing on how chemical engineering could reduce the impact of such gases – an early environmental initiative – Davis published a number of works that include *A Handbook of Chemical Engineering*.

Instrumental in 1881 in the formation of the Society of Chemical Industry, he died in 1906, while the George E. David Medal of the Institution of Chemical Engineers is named in his honour.

From science to the world of politics, Jefferson Davis served as President of the Confederate States of America during the American Civil War of 1861 to 1865.

Born in 1808 in Kentucky of mixed English and Welsh descent, he fought in the Mexican-American War of 1846 to 1848 and, as a Democratic Party senator of Mississippi, from 1853 to 1857 as U.S. Secretary of War.

Operator of a cotton plantation in Mississippi and the owner of more than 100 slaves, he was opposed to the abolition of slavery and, accordingly, supported the secession of the Confederate states from the Union.

Inaugurated shortly before the outbreak of the civil war as President of the Confederacy, he was imprisoned for a time after its defeat.

He died in 1889, while memorials to him include an obelisk at the Jefferson Davis State Historic Site in Fairview, Kentucky and a memorial on Monument Avenue, Richmond, Virginia.

In contemporary British politics, David Davis is the British Conservative Party politician born to a single mother in York in 1948 and raised on a council estate in Tooting, southwest London.

A graduate of a number of institutions that include Warwick University, the London Business School and Harvard University and having worked for a time as a senior executive with Tate & Lyle, he was first elected to Parliament in 1987 as MP for the Boothferry constituency.

He resigned from his seat in June of 2008 to force a by-election in order to provoke a debate over what he perceived was an erosion of civil liberties – and was subsequently re-elected.

Having held senior posts including Minister of State for Europe from 1994 to 1997 and chairman of the Conservative Party from 2001 to 2002, he was appointed Secretary of State for Exiting the European Union in July of 2016.

But he resigned two years later in protest over Prime Minister Theresa May's exit plan.

One bearer of the Davis name with a rather macabre claim to fame was Edwin F. Davis, who invented many of the features of the American instrument of judicial execution known as the electric chair.

Born in 1846 in Corning, Steuben County,

New York, he became the first "state electrician", or executioner, for New York State and between 1890 and 1914 carried out 240 executions in the notorious Sing Sing Prison in the Hudson Valley.

These include, on August 6, 1890, William Kemmler, the first person to be electrocuted by means of what is macabrely known as 'Old Sparky', for the murder of his common-law wife.

On March 20, 1899, Martha M. Place became the first female victim of the chair when she was executed for the murder of her stepdaughter, while on October 9, 1901 Davis supervised the execution of Leon Frank Czolgosz, the assassin of William McKinley, 25th President of the United States.

Holding U.S. Patent No. 587,649 for his "Electrocution-Chair", Davis died in 1923.

On a rather spooky footnote, in 2007 it was reported a couple living in what had been his home in New York were experiencing a series of paranormal activities that included mysterious 'bumps in the night' and apparitions.

Chapter four:

On the world stage

An icon of the silver screen and a two-time Academy Award winner, Ruth Elizabeth Davis was the American actress better known as Bette Davis.

Ranked second, next to Katherine Hepburn, in the American Film Institute's list of "50 Greatest American Screen Legends" and born in 1908 in Lowell, Massachusetts of mixed English and French-Canadian descent, it was when she was aged 20 that she made her Broadway debut in the play *Broken Dishes*.

Hollywood beckoned, and in 1930 she was screen tested for Universal Studios but failed.

Passing another screen test a year later, and with the cinematographer Karl Freund impressed by her "lovely eyes", she was cast that year in the film *Bad Sister*.

Later signed to Warner Brothers, her early credits include the 1932 *The Man Who Played God*, the 1934 *Of Human Bondage* and the 1935 *Dangerous*, for which she won an Academy Award for Best Actress.

Further major credits throughout the 1930s include the 1936 *The Petrified Forest*, co-starring with Humphrey Bogart and Leslie Howard, the 1938 *Jezebel*, which netted her another Academy Award for Best Actress, and the 1939 *Dark Victory*, for which she was nominated for an Academy Award for Best Actress.

Credits throughout the 1940s – with the actress frequently filmed in close-up to emphasise her startlingly distinctive eyes – include the 1940 *All This and Heaven Too*, the 1940 *The Letter*, the 1942 *New Voyager* and, from 1948, *Winter Meeting*.

Film credits throughout the 1950s include the 1951 *Payment on Demand* and, from the same year, *Another Man's Poison*, while in the 1960s, starring beside Joan Crawford, she received another Academy Award nomination for Best Actress for her role of Baby Jane Hudson in the 1962 *What Ever Happened to Baby Jane?*

Appointed the first ever female president of the Academy of Motion Pictures Arts and Sciences in 1941 and the recipient in 1977 of the American Film Institute's Lifetime Achievement Award, film credits towards the end of her career include the 1978 *Death on the Nile*, the 1978 *Return to Witch Mountain* and, from 1980, *The Watcher in the Woods*.

Nominated for an Emmy Award for her role in the 1979 television mini-series *Strangers: The Story of a Mother and Daughter*, she was immortalised in song in 1981 with the singer Kim Carnes' international hit *Bette Davis Eyes*, written by Jackie Deshannon.

Married four times, widowed once and divorced thrice, she died in 1989, while the United States Postal Service issued a commemorative postage stamp in her honour in 2008 to mark the centenary of her birth.

An all-round entertainer, **Sammy Davis Jr.** was the American singer, actor and impressionist born Samuel George Davis Jr. in Harlem, New York City, in 1925.

The son of an African-American entertainer, Sammy Davis Sr. and Elvira Sanchez, a tap dancer of Afro-Cuban descent, the future Hollywood star first took to the stage as a child with his father and family friend Will Mastin in the dance act the Will Mastin Trio.

Serving in the Second World War with an entertainment Special Services unit, Davis rejoined the dance act at the end of the conflict and later, as a singer, began recording.

Singing the title track for the 1954 film *Six Bridges to Cross* and starring two years later in the Broadway play *Mr Wonderful*, he became a member three years after that, along with fellow entertainers Frank Sinatra, Dean Martin, Peter Lawford and Joey Bishop, of what the media dubbed the 'Rat Pack.'

Films credited to the Rat Pack are the 1960 *Oceans 11*, the 1962 *Sergeants 3* and, from 1964, *Robin and the 7 Hoods*, while in 1972 Davis enjoyed international chart success with the song *Candy Man*.

Meanwhile performing at the Frontier Casino in Las Vegas – where he became famed for his impersonations, particularly of fellow entertainers – he also had television credits that include *I Dream of Jeannie*, *All in the Family* and *Charlie's Angels*.

In 1954 he lost his left eye after the vehicle he was travelling in was involved in a collision, while in 1961 the entertainer – whose father was Protestant and mother Catholic – formally converted to the Jewish faith.

Romantically and controversially involved for a brief period – mixed race relationships condemned by racists – with the actress Kim Novak and married for a time to the dancer Loray White and then the actress May Britt, he married the dancer Altovise Gore in 1970.

Prominent in the American Civil Rights movement, in 1973 Davis and his wife were invited by President Richard Nixon to sleep overnight in the White House – the first African-Americans so invited.

The recipient of the Kennedy Center Honors in 1987, he died in 1990, in substantial debt to the Internal Revenue Service.

The lights of the Las Vegas Strip were darkened for ten minutes in tribute to him two days after his death, while in 2001 he was posthumously awarded a Grammy Lifetime Achievement Award.

In contemporary times, **Kristin Davis** is the American actress best known for her role from 1998 to 2004 of Charlotte York Goldenblatt on television's *Sex and the City*.

Born in 1965 in Boulder, Colorado, other television credits include *Melrose Place*, while big screen credits include the 2006 *Deck the Halls*, the 2008 *Sex and the City: The Movie* and, from 2010, *Sex and the City 2*.

Best known for his role from 1978 until his death in 1981 of Jock Ewing in the internationally popular television soap *Dallas*, Marlin Davis was the American actor better known by his stage name of **Jim Davis**.

Born in 1909 in Edgerton, Platte County, Missouri, he appeared on the big screen beside Bette Davis in the 1948 *Winter Meeting*, while other television credits include the Westerns *Gunsmoke*, *High Chaparral* and *Laramie*.

Winner of the 1988 Academy Award for Best Supporting Actress for her role in *The Accidental Tourist*, **Geena Davis** is the American actress, writer, producer and former fashion model born in 1956 in Wareham, Massachusetts.

Also nominated for an Academy Award for Best Actress along with co-star Susan Sarandon for her performance in the 1991 *Thelma and Louise*, her other screen credits include the 1986 *The Fly*, the 1996 *The Long Kiss Goodnight* and, from 1999, *Stuart Little*.

On British shores, **Warwick Davis** is the actor, writer, television director and producer born in 1970 in Epsom, Surrey.

Born with a rare form of dwarfism, he was cast as the Ewok Wicket in the 1983 *Star Wars Episode VI: Return of the Jedi*, while he also appears in the 2015 *Star Wars: The Force Awakens*, the 1988 *Willow* and the *Harry Potter* series of films.

With other film credits that include the 1993 *Leprechaun*, his television credits include *The Chronicles of Narnia* and the sitcom *Life's Too Short*, where he plays a fictionalised version of himself.

Born in 1962 in Malvern, Worcestershire, **Evan Davis** is the British journalist, economist, radio and television presenter who in 2018 was appointed lead presenter of BBC Radio 4's flagship *PM* programme.

Main host from 2014 to 2018 of the BBC's *Newsnight* television programme, having replaced Jeremy Paxton, since 2015 he has also fronted *Dragon's Den*, where would-be entrepreneurs hoping for investment present their ideas.

Bearers of the Davis name have also excelled in the highly competitive world of sport – no less so than on the snooker table with the brothers Joe and Fred Davis and fellow champion Steve Davis.

Born in 1913 in Chesterfield, Derbyshire, **Fred Davis** was the winner of the World Snooker Championship in 1948, 1949 and 1951 and the World Billiards Championship in 1969.

Awarded the OBE in 1977, he died in 1998.

Posthumously inducted into the Snooker Hall of Fame in 2011, he was the younger brother of **Joe Davis**, born in 1901.

Winner of the World Billiards Championship in 1928, 1930 and 1932, he was instrumental in organising the first snooker World Championship in 1927, which he won. Dominating the game by winning the championship every year from 1927 to 1940, he entered the snooker history records in 1955 in an exhibition match at Leicester Square Hall, London, by achieving the first officially recognised maximum break of 147.

Also a recipient of an OBE, he died in 1978.

Sharing the same surname but not related to Fred and Joe, **Steve Davis** is the English professional player who throughout the 1980s won the World Championship six times.

Born in 1957 in Plumstead, London and ranked the world number one snooker player for seven consecutive seasons, he completed the game's Triple Crown during the 1987/1988 season – the first to do so – by winning the UK Championship, the Masters and the World Championship.

Still active as a player, he is also a popular BBC television pundit while, also accomplished in the highly cerebral game of chess and a former president of the British Chess Federation, he has co-authored books on the game in addition to writing a number of books on cricket and his other passion of cooking.

From the snooker table to the tennis court, **Dwight Filley Davis** was the American player and politician who at the turn of the twentieth century founded the international tennis competition now known as the Davis Cup.

Born in 1879 in St Louis, Missouri, he was the winner along with Holcombe Ward of the U.S. Men's Doubles championship from 1899 to 1901 and a runner-up along with Ward in the 1901 Men's Doubles final at Wimbledon.

In 1901 he laid the foundations for the International Lawn Tennis Challenge – later renamed the Davis Cup in his honour – and, along with three others, designing and donating a silver cup for the winners; he died in 1945, after having served as U.S. Secretary of War from 1925 to 1929.

In the world of music, Miles Dewey Davis III was the jazz legend better known as **Miles Davis**.

Born in 1926 in Alton, Illinois, the trumpeter, bandleader and composer first picked up the trumpet when he was aged thirteen.

He went on to produce a series of seminal works that include the 1959 album *Kind of Blue* – the best-selling jazz album of all time – the 1970 *Bitches Brew* and the 1985 *You're Under Arrest*.

The recipient of numerous accolades that include eight Grammy awards, three Grammy Hall of Fame Awards and a Grammy Lifetime Achievement Award and recognised as having had a profound influence on not only jazz but also rock music, the highly innovative musician died in 1991.

A composer and conductor famed for his television and film scores, **Carl Davis** was born in New York City in 1936, but took up residence in the United Kingdom in 1961.

A conductor with the London Philharmonic Orchestra and occasionally the Royal Liverpool Philharmonic Orchestra, he has written scores for British television productions that include the 1975 *The Naked Civil Servant*, the 1984 *The Far Pavilions* and the 1973 series *The World at War*.

The recipient of a CBE, his film score credits include the 1981 *The French Lieutenant's Woman* – for which he won a BAFTA Award for Best Film Music, the 2000 *The Great Gatsby* and, from 2008, *The Understudy*.